$\mathcal{P}$ROCLAIM $\mathcal{P}$RAISE

Daily Prayer for Parish and Home

An Order of Prayer for
Mornings and Evenings for
Each Day of the Week with
Midday Prayers and
Night Prayers

Ⓐcknowledgments

Excerpts from the English translation of *The Liturgy of the Hours* © 1974, International Committee on English in the Liturgy, Inc. (ICEL); excerpts from the English translation of *A Book of Prayers* © 1982, ICEL; the English translation of the psalms and canticles from the *Liturgical Psalter* © 1994, ICEL; text of some of the intercessions from *Daily Praise: A Study of Morning, Evening, and Night Prayer* © 1995, ICEL. All rights reserved.

This book was designed by Jill Smith. Psalm prayers were written by Gabe Huck. Karen Nicholls set the type in Palatino, Gill Sans and Linoscript. Jennifer McGeary provided editorial assistance. It was printed at Arcata Graphics Company. Printed in the United States of America.

Library of Congress Cataloging-in-Publication Data
Proclaim praise : Daily prayer for parish and home : an order of prayer for
    mornings and evenings for each day of the week, with midday prayers
    and night prayers.
        129 p.
        1. Catholic Church —Prayer-books and devotions — English.
2. Bible. O.T. Psalms — Devotional use. 3. Devotional calendars.
I. Huck, Gabe
BX2130.p76 1994   93-29357
264′ .028   CIP

ISBN 0-929650-94-8
PRAYER

Contents

INTRODUCTION

People of the church have from the beginning marked the morning and the evening with prayer. Song and psalms and scripture have been part of this time. This book is intended to help those Christians who would continue this tradition. It offers a way to pray with and as the church. It is a simple way to let the psalms become ours again, and so let them teach us to pray.

This book is a short form of the church's Morning Prayer, Evening Prayer and Night Prayer. It includes psalms for Midday Prayer and blessings at table.

This book is intended especially for the various groups that meet in parishes. Individuals or members of a household praying together or other small groups will also find it useful.

The form of this prayer, taken from the Liturgy of the Hours, is quite simple:
• an introductory verse
• a hymn appropriate to the morning or evening

- a psalm
- silence and a prayer that concludes the psalm
- a reading from scripture
- the canticle from the gospels
- prayers of intercession
- the Lord's Prayer
- a concluding verse

The foundation of this way of praying is the introductory verse, the psalm, silence, the Lord's Prayer and the concluding verse. The other elements are included as time allows, but a Christian's daily prayer has always given an important place to prayers of intercession.

The psalms for each day are chosen from those assigned to that day in the Liturgy of the Hours. In every use, even when a person prays alone, the pace should be peaceful and attentive.

Praying at Home

It is better to simplify than to hurry. Sometimes these prayers can be used at the time of the evening meal, praying the hymn and psalm before the meal, then reading scripture and praying the intercessions afterward.

Praying in the Small Group

A group using this form of prayer would ask one person to lead and another to read the scripture.

The person who reads the scripture should have an opportunity beforehand to prepare. The Bible should be treated with reverence; in some cases, a candle burning by the Bible would be appropriate at Evening Prayer. The candle is lighted just before the group begins to pray.

The leader of prayer begins and ends the prayer by speaking the first part of the appropriate verse (e.g., "Lord, open my lips") to which all those present respond. After the psalm, the leader addresses the invitation "Let us pray" to the group and, after some moments of silence, reads the prayer. The leader may introduce the prayers of intercession; this will usually be an invitation for all to speak aloud their prayers (or the prayers of those present can be combined with general prayers like those found on page 101 and following). When the intercessions are finished, the leader begins the Lord's Prayer.

The leader serves well when he or she is familiar with the whole order of the prayer and attentive to preparing the prayer after the psalm and other spoken texts.

Even when one of these prayers is used at the beginning of a parish meeting, the pace should not be hurried. When the hour is late, as at the end of an evening meeting, the Night Prayer may be chosen.

A small group may stand for the whole time of prayer, or they may stand at the beginning, be seated for the psalm and scripture, and stand again until the conclusion. It may sometimes be appropriate to kneel for the prayers of intercession.

The Song and Psalm

With one exception, the songs that have been included may be sung to many familiar tunes (for example: the tune called Old Hundredth; "Praise God from whom all blessings flow"). The hymn for Sunday Morning Prayer is the only one that has a different meter. For those who use this form of prayer frequently, additional hymns appropriate to the hours of the day should be sought out.

Copies of this book are needed by all those present so that all may join in the hymn and psalm. When a group prays a psalm or the gospel canticle, two sides of the room may alternate stanzas. In this book, no stanza is split between the bottom of one page and the top of another. Thus a new page always means a new stanza of the psalm or canticle.

The psalms themselves have been the constant prayers of Jews and of Christians. They are the texts that teach us to pray, the texts that join our prayers to the prayers of our ancestors and of our children. Today the psalms have again become the daily prayers of many. This translation seeks to be faithful to the original text by speaking in direct and strong language.

The Scripture Reading
The reading from scripture could be chosen from the lectionary for Mass or from the Liturgy of the Hours.

However, an individual using this prayer or a group that prays together regularly may wish instead to read in order through various books of the Bible, reading shorter or longer passages each day depending on the time available and the desire of the group.

In a group, the reading may be introduced, as at the Sunday liturgy, by saying: "A reading from . . ." And it may be concluded by saying: "The word of the Lord," to which all may respond, "Thanks be to God." Some moments of silence are fitting after the reading from scripture.

SUNDAY MORNING

Make the sign of the cross and say:

Lord, open my lips.
And my mouth will proclaim your praise.

This hymn or another hymn is sung.

On this day, the first of days,
God the maker's name we praise;
Who, creation's Lord and spring,
Did the world from darkness bring.

Word-made-flesh, all praises be!
You from sin have set us free;
And with you we die and rise
Unto God in sacrifice.

Holy Spirit, you impart
Gifts of love to ev'ry heart;
Give us light and grace, we pray,
Fill our hearts this holy day.

Psalm 63

God, my God, you I crave;
my soul thirsts for you,
my body aches for you
like a dry and weary land.
Let me gaze on you in your temple:
a vision of strength and glory.

Your love is better than life,
my speech is full of praise.
I give you a lifetime of worship,
my hands raised in your name.
I feast at a rich table,
my lips sing of your glory.

On my bed I lie awake,
your memory fills the night.
You have been my help,
I rejoice beneath your wings.
Yes, I cling to you,
your right hand holds me fast.

Let those who want me dead
end up deep in the grave!
They will die by the sword,
their bodies food for jackals.
But let the king find joy in God.
All who swear the truth be praised,
every lying mouth be shut.

Let us pray.

After a time of silence:

We cling to each other, God,
you and this people,
believing in each other, sheltering each other,
each the other's dream, each the other's dear love.
So be both thirst and its sweet relief,
be hunger and be the welcome table,
the table of this Sunday,
the table where we shall belong to each other
for ever and ever.
Amen.

A passage from scripture may be read here, followed by a time of silence.

The Canticle of Zechariah may be recited or sung (page 114).

Then intercessions are made. If appropriate, all may respond to each intercession: "Lord, have mercy," or "Lord, hear our prayer." Examples of prayers of intercession are found on page 101 and following.

Then the Lord's Prayer is recited or sung.

In conclusion make the sign of the cross and say:

May the Lord bless us,
protect us from all evil,
and bring us to everlasting life.
Amen.

SUNDAY EVENING

After lighting a candle (if possible), make the sign of the cross and say:

God, come to my assistance.
Lord, make haste to me.

This hymn or another hymn is sung.

O radiant light, O sun divine
Of God the Father's deathless face,
O image of the light sublime
That fills the heav'nly dwelling place.

O Son of God, the source of life,
Praise is your due by night and day:
Our happy lips must raise the strain
Of your esteemed and splendid name.

Lord Jesus Christ, as daylight fades,
As shine the lights of eventide,
We praise the Father with the Son,
The Spirit blest and with them one.

Psalm 114

Israel marches out of Egypt,
Jacob leaves an alien people.
Judah becomes a holy place,
Israel, God's domain.

The sea pulls back for them,
the Jordan flees in retreat.
Mountains jump like rams,
hills like lambs in fear.

Why shrink back, O sea?
Jordan, why recoil?
Why shudder, mountains, like rams?
Why quiver, hills, like lambs?

Tremble! earth, before the Lord,
before the God of Jacob,
who turns rock to water,
flint to gushing streams.

Let us pray.

After a time of silence:

For rivers running back and forth,
springs flowing out of flint,
simple pools of water:
we praise you, God of Jacob!
You call Israel to cross the sea to your side —
and all creation leaps!
You call us, who were once far off,
to come near on this day
and be washed in the blood of the lamb,
your own Lamb, lifted on the cross,
Jesus, our Lord for ever and ever.
Amen.

A passage from scripture may be read here, followed by a time of silence.

The Canticle of Mary may be recited or sung (page 116).

Then intercessions are made. If appropriate, all may respond to each intercession: "Lord, have mercy," or "Lord, hear our prayer." Examples of prayers of intercession are found on page 101 and following.

Then the Lord's Prayer is recited or sung.

Make the sign of the cross and say:

May the Lord bless us,
protect us from all evil,
and bring us to everlasting life.
Amen.

MONDAY MORNING

Make the sign of the cross and say:

Lord, open my lips.
And my mouth will proclaim your praise.

This hymn or another hymn is sung.

Now that the daylight fills the sky,
We lift our hearts to God on high,
That God in all we do or say,
Would keep us free from harm today.

So we, when this day's work is o'er,
And shades of night return once more,
Our path of trial safely trod,
Shall give the glory to our God.

All praise to God the Father be,
And praise the Son eternally,
Whom with the Spirit we adore,
One God alone, for evermore.

Psalm 5

Hear my words, my groans,
my cries for help,
O God my king.
I pray to you, Lord,
my prayer rises with the sun.
At dawn I plead my case and wait.

You never welcome evil, God,
never let it stay.
You hate arrogance
and abhor scoundrels,
you detest violence
and destroy the traitor.

But by your great mercy
I enter your house
and bend low in awe
within your holy temple.

In the face of my enemies
clear the way,
bring me your justice.

Their charges are groundless,
they breathe destruction;
their tongues are smooth,
their throat an open grave.

God, pronounce them guilty,
catch them in their own plots,
expel them for their sins;
they have betrayed you.

But let those who trust you
be glad and celebrate for ever.
Protect those who love your name,
then they will delight in you.

For you bless the just, O God,
your grace surrounds them like a shield.

Let us pray

After a time of silence:

Silent God,
as earth spins dawn to one place after another,
every moment begins a day never known before.
Let morning's light signal your mercy to those
    who cry,
let it signal your struggle against evil taken up
    once more.
Let the light signal too your joyful love
for the earth itself and all its elements,
the vegetation, the great numbers of animals,
and among these ourselves, the just and the unjust,
who all live by your grace,
you who are blessed now and for ever.
Amen.

A passage from scripture may be read here, followed by a time of silence.

The Canticle of Zechariah may be recited or sung (page 114).

Then intercessions are made. If appropriate, all may respond to each intercession: "Lord, have mercy," or "Lord, hear our prayer." Examples of prayers of intercession are found on page 101 and following.

Then the Lord's Prayer is recited or sung.

In conclusion make the sign of the cross and say:

May the Lord bless us,
protect us from all evil,
and bring us to everlasting life.
Amen.

MONDAY EVENING

After lighting a candle (if possible), make the sign of the cross and say:

God, come to my assistance.
Lord, make haste to me.

This hymn or another hymn is sung.

O splendor of eternal light,
Who in full glory dwell on high!
The world began as light from light,
All goodness in the Father's sight.

Upon the twilight chaos played,
Your Wisdom forming night and day.
As night descends to you we sing
To hover near on brooding wing.

Let heaven's Spirit pulse within
To purge the memory of sin;
Thus, casting off forgetful night,
We rise enrobed with firstborn light.

Psalm 124

Say it, Israel!
If the Lord had not been with us,
if the Lord had not been for us
when enemies rose against us,
they would have swallowed us
in their blazing anger,
and the raging waters
would have swept us away—
rushing, surging water,
thundering over us.

Blessed be the Lord
for saving our flesh from their teeth,
for tearing the trapper's net,
so we could flutter away like birds.
Our help is the Lord,
creator of earth and sky.

Let us pray

After a time of silence:

Raging waters have brought terror and salvation for us,
blessed God:
from the time they stood as a wall to the left
and a wall to the right
and Moses and Miriam led the slavery-ending
    procession through,
until these times
when we ourselves have passed through the waters
    of baptism.
Let our song of victory be only:
If God had not been with us!
Blessed are you, Lord our God, for ever and ever.
Amen.

*A passage from scripture may be read here, followed by a time
of silence.*

The Canticle of Mary may be recited or sung (page 116).

Then intercessions are made. If appropriate, all may respond to each intercession: "Lord, have mercy," or "Lord, hear our prayer." Examples of prayers of intercession are found on page 101 and following.

Then the Lord's Prayer is recited or sung.

Make the sign of the cross and say:

May the Lord bless us,
protect us from all evil,
and bring us to everlasting life.
Amen.

TUESDAY MORNING

Make the sign of the cross and say:

Lord, open my lips.
And my mouth will proclaim your praise.

This hymn or another hymn is sung.

Great Lord of splendor, source of light,
Your gentle rays dispel the night
Whose reign of darkness yields to dawn,
Then dies in blaze of rising sun.

Lord Jesus, day star from on high,
Your rising heralds in the dawn;
True morning star which never sets,
Come, shed your light on humankind.

More radiant than ten thousand suns,
True light enlight'ning ev'ry one,
Shine in the darkness of our hearts;
Come with your healing grace and truth.

Psalm 85

Lord, you loved your land,
brought Jacob back,
forgot our guilt,
forgave our sins,
swallowed your anger,
your blazing anger.

Bring us back,
saving God.
End your wrath.
Will it stop,
or drag on for ever?

Turn, revive us,
nourish our joy.
Show us mercy,
Save us, Lord!

I listen to God speaking:
"I, the Lord, speak peace,
peace to my faithful people
who turn their hearts to me."
Salvation is coming near,
glory is filling our land.

Love and fidelity embrace,
peace and justice kiss.
Fidelity sprouts from the earth,
justice leans down from heaven.

The Lord pours out riches,
our land springs to life.
Justice clears God's path,
justice points the way.

Let us pray.

After a time of silence:

Rightly do you rage against us,
God whose glory is justice!
From one generation to another
we have made ourselves at home in exile,
at home with dreariness and misery.
We do not even miss your beauty.
But shake us awake, young and old,
awake and hungry to see justice done
and to recognize, at last, the beauty that dwells among us.
You are our God for ever and ever.
Amen.

*A passage from scripture may be read here, followed by a time
of silence.*

The Canticle of Zechariah may be recited or sung (page 114).

Then intercessions are made. If appropriate, all may respond to each intercession: "Lord, have mercy," or "Lord, hear our prayer." Examples of prayers of intercession are found on page 101 and following.

Then the Lord's Prayer is recited or sung.

In conclusion make the sign of the cross and say:

May the Lord bless us,
protect us from all evil,
and bring us to everlasting life.
Amen.

TUESDAY EVENING

After lighting a candle (if possible), make the sign of the cross and say:

God, come to my assistance.
Lord, make haste to me

This hymn or another hymn is sung.

Lord Jesus Christ, abide with us,
Now that the sun has run its course;
Let hope not be obscured by night
But may faith's darkness be as light.

Lord Jesus Christ, grant us your peace,
And when the trials of earth shall cease;
Grant us the morning light of grace,
The radiant splendor of your face.

Immortal, holy, threefold light,
Yours be the kingdom, pow'r and might;
All glory be eternally
To you, life-giving Trinity.

Psalm 137

By the rivers of Babylon
we sat weeping,
remembering Zion.
There on the poplars
we hung our harps.

Our captors shouted
for happy songs,
for songs of festival.
"Sing!" they cried,
"the songs of Zion."

How could we sing
the song of the Lord
in a foreign land?

Jerusalem forgotten?
Wither my hand!
Jerusalem forgotten?
Silence my voice!
if I do not seek you
as my greatest joy.

Lord, never forget
that crime of Edom
against your city,
the day they cried,
"Strip! Smash her to the ground!"

Doomed Babylon, be cursed!
Good for those who deal you
evil for evil!
Good for those who destroy you,
who smash your children at the walls.

Let us pray.

After a time of silence:

God of our never-seen homeland,
day by day, we remember:
We are exiles and this place is not our home.
Here we cannot join the songs sung to other gods,
nor can we sing of you as we will one day
when you remember us and bring us home.
Even if you forget us,
we and our children will clamor endlessly:
Remember us, Lord, remember us for ever.
Amen.

A passage from scripture may be read here, followed by a time of silence.

The Canticle of Mary may be recited or sung (page 116).

Then intercessions are made. If appropriate, all may respond to each intercession: "Lord, have mercy," or "Lord, hear our prayer." Examples of prayers of intercession are found on page 101 and following.

Then the Lord's Prayer is recited or sung.

Make the sign of the cross and say:

May the Lord bless us,
protect us from all evil,
and bring us to everlasting life.
Amen.

WEDNESDAY MORNING

Make the sign of the cross and say:

Lord, open my lips.
And my mouth will proclaim your praise.

This hymn or another hymn is sung.

Now that the daylight fills the sky,
We lift our hearts to God on high,
That God in all we do or say,
Would keep us free from harm today.

O may our inmost heart be pure,
From thoughts of folly kept secure,
And all our powers devoted be
To deeds of love that keep us free.

All praise to God the Father be,
And praise the Son eternally,
Whom with the Spirit we adore,
One God alone, for evermore.

Psalm 146

Praise the Lord, my heart!
My whole life, give praise.
Let me sing to God
as long as I live.

Never depend on rulers:
born of earth, they cannot save.
They die, they turn to dust.
That day, their plans crumble.

They are wise who depend on God,
who look to Jacob's Lord,
creator of heaven and earth,
maker of the teeming sea.

The Lord keeps faith for ever,
giving food to the hungry,
justice to the poor,
freedom to captives.

The Lord opens blind eyes
and straightens the bent,
comforting widows and orphans,
protecting the stranger.
The Lord loves the just
but blocks the path of the wicked.

Zion, praise the Lord!
Your God reigns for ever,
from generation to generation.
Hallelujah!

Let us pray.

After a time of silence:

We look for you, Jacob's Lord,
where rulers are brought low,
where the poor have justice at last,
where every sorrow finds compassion,
where strangers are welcomed at table.

But when such blessed deeds seem overwhelmed
by the evil that is so casual, so constant,
then make us depend all the more on you,
the only Lord, for ever and ever.
Amen.

A passage from scripture may be read here, followed by a time of silence.

The Canticle of Zechariah may be recited or sung (page 114).

Then intercessions are made. If appropriate, all may respond to each intercession: "Lord, have mercy," or "Lord, hear our prayer." Examples of prayers of intercession are found on page 101 and following.

Then the Lord's Prayer is recited or sung.

In conclusion make the sign of the cross and say:

May the Lord bless us,
protect us from all evil,
and bring us to everlasting life.
Amen.

WEDNESDAY EVENING

After lighting a candle (if possible), make the sign of the cross and say:

God, come to my assistance.
Lord, make haste to me.

This hymn or another hymn is sung.

We praise you, Father, for your gift
Of dusk and nightfall over earth,
Foreshadowing the mystery
Of death that leads to endless day.

Within your hands we rest secure;
In quiet sleep our strength renew;
Yet give your people hearts that wake
In love to you, unsleeping Lord.

Your glory may we ever seek
In rest, as in activity,
Until its fullness is revealed,
O source of life, O Trinity.

Psalm 126

The Lord brings us back to Zion,
we are like dreamers,
laughing, dancing,
with songs on our lips.

Other nations say,
"A new world of wonders!
The Lord is with them."
Yes, God works wonders.
Rejoice! Be glad!

Lord, bring us back
as water to thirsty land.
Those sowing in tears
reap, singing and laughing.

They left weeping, weeping,
casting the seed.
They come back singing, singing,
holding high the harvest.

Let us pray.

After a time of silence:

What tears you cry, sower God, over us all.
But how you laugh in amazement
and what songs you sing
when there is some harvest.
Your saints from Adam and Eve,
from Moses and Miriam,
until our own grandparents and parents,
and we too,
need your tears
and long to hear your laughter.
Harvest us home to sing your praise
for ever and ever.
Amen.

*A passage from scripture may be read here, followed by a time
of silence.*

The Canticle of Mary may be recited or sung (page 116).

Then intercessions are made. If appropriate, all may respond to each intercession: "Lord, have mercy," or "Lord, hear our prayer." Examples of prayers of intercession are found on page 101 and following.

Then the Lord's Prayer is recited or sung.

Make the sign of the cross and say:

May the Lord bless us,
protect us from all evil,
and bring us to everlasting life.
Amen.

THURSDAY MORNING

Make the sign of the cross and say:

Lord, open my lips.
And my mouth will proclaim your praise.

This hymn or another hymn is sung.

Awake, be lifted up, O heart,
And with the angels bear your part,
Who all night long unwearied sing
High praise to the eternal king.

All praise to you who safe have kept
And have refreshed us while we slept;
Grant, Lord, when we from death shall wake,
We may of endless light partake.

Direct, control, suggest, this day,
All we design, or do, or say;
That all our pow'rs, with all their might,
In your sole glory may unite.

Psalm 143

Hear me, faithful Lord!
bend to my prayer,
show compassion.
Do not judge me harshly;
in your sight, no one is just.

My enemy hunts me down,
grinding me to dust,
caging me with the dead
in lasting darkness.
My strength drains away,
my heart is numb.

I remember the ancient days,
I recall your wonders,
the work of your hands.
Dry as thirsty land,
I reach out for you.

Answer me quickly, Lord.
My strength is spent.
Do not hide from me
or I will fall into the grave.

Let morning announce your love,
for it is you I trust.
Show me the right way,
I offer you myself.

Rescue me from my foes,
you are my only refuge, Lord.
Teach me your will,
for you are my God.

Graciously lead me, Lord,
on to level ground.
I call on your just name,
keep me safe, free from danger.

In your great love for me,
disarm my enemies,
destroy their power,
for I belong to you.

Let us pray.

After a time of silence:

Blessed God,
our whole world could voice such fear:
We are hunted down by enemies never dreamed
      about before;
the world and its very soil are worn down;
But there is morning, morning like your promise,
like your covenant.
When there is nothing else, teach us to wait
and to call on your name
till even death is defeated
and we are with you for ever and ever.
Amen.

A passage from scripture may be read here, followed by a time of silence.

The Canticle of Zechariah may be recited or sung (page 114).

Then intercessions are made. If appropriate, all may respond to each intercession: "Lord, have mercy," or "Lord, hear our prayer." Examples of prayers of intercession are found on page 101 and following.

Then the Lord's Prayer is recited or sung.

In conclusion make the sign of the cross and say:

May the Lord bless us,
protect us from all evil,
and bring us to everlasting life.
Amen.

THURSDAY EVENING

After lighting a candle (if possible), make the sign of the cross and say:

God, come to my assistance.
Lord, make haste to me.

This hymn or another hymn is sung.

O splendor of eternal light,
Who in full glory dwell on high!
The world began as light from light,
All goodness in the Father's sight.

Upon the twilight chaos played,
Your Wisdom forming night and day.
As night descends to you we sing
To hover near on brooding wing.

Let heaven's Spirit pulse within
To purge the memory of sin;
Thus, casting off forgetful night,
We rise enrobed with firstborn light.

Psalm 32

Happy the pardoned,
whose sin is canceled,
in whom God finds
no evil, no deceit.

While I hid my sin,
my bones grew weak
from endless groaning.

Day and night,
under the weight of your hand,
my strength withered
as in a summer drought.

Then I stopped hiding my sin
and spoke out,
"God, I confess my wrong."
And you pardoned me.

No wonder the faithful
pray to you in danger!
Even a sudden flood
will never touch them.

You, my shelter,
you save me from ruin.
You encircle me
with songs of freedom.

"I show you the path to walk.
As your teacher,
I watch out for you.

"Do not be a stubborn mule,
needing bridle and bit
to be tamed."
Evil brings grief;
trusting in God brings love.

Rejoice in the Lord.
Be glad and sing,
you faithful and just.

Let us pray.

After a time of silence:

Encircle us, God, with freedom's songs.
Teach us, the pardoned, to sing the songs of angels.
Catch up all the groaning of this earth,
all its sadness, all its weight,
into that grace that we can sing but cannot yet know.
You shall be our home for ever and ever.
Amen.

*A passage from scripture may be read here, followed by a time
of silence.*

The Canticle of Mary may be recited or sung (page 116).

Then intercessions are made. If appropriate, all may respond to each intercession: "Lord, have mercy," or "Lord, hear our prayer." Examples of prayers of intercession are found on page 101 and following.

Then the Lord's Prayer is recited or sung.

Make the sign of the cross and say:

May the Lord bless us,
protect us from all evil,
and bring us to everlasting life.
Amen.

FRIDAY MORNING

Make the sign of the cross and say:

Lord, open my lips.
And my mouth will proclaim your praise.

This hymn or another hymn is sung.

We bless you, Father, Lord of life,
To whom all living beings tend,
The source of holiness and grace,
Our first beginning and our end.

We give you thanks, redeeming Christ,
Who bore our weight of sin and shame;
In dark defeat, you conquered sin,
And death, by dying, overcame.

Come, Holy Spirit, searching fire,
Whose flame all evil burns away,
With light and love come down to us
In silence and in peace to stay.

Psalm 51

Have mercy, tender God,
forget that I defied you.
Wash away my sin,
cleanse me from my guilt.

I know my evil well,
it stares me in the face,
evil done to you alone
before your very eyes.

How right your condemnation!
Your verdict clearly just.
You see me for what I am,
a sinner before my birth.

You love those centered in truth;
teach me your hidden wisdom.
Wash me with fresh water,
wash me bright as snow.

Fill me with happy songs,
let the bones you bruised now dance.
Shut your eyes to my sin,
make my guilt disappear.

Creator, reshape my heart,
God, steady my spirit.
Do not cast me aside
stripped of your holy spirit.

Save me, bring back my joy,
support me, strengthen my will.
Then I will teach your way
and sinners will turn to you.

Help me, stop my tears,
and I will sing your goodness.
Lord, give me words
and I will shout your praise.

When I offer a holocaust,
the gift does not please you.
So I offer my shattered spirit;
a changed heart you welcome.

In your love make Zion lovely,
rebuild the walls of Jerusalem.
Then sacrifice will please you,
young bulls upon your altar.

Let us pray.

After a time of silence:

Tender God,
seldom heard but ever persisting,
your word warns the powerful,
all of us whose choices this day
will bind and limit others.
Give us clear sight to know our sins
and tears to weep for such a world.

Wrap us round with mercy
that forgiven we may forgive
and loved we may love.
Mercy, God, for mercy is yours
now and for ever.
Amen.

A passage from scripture may be read here, followed by a time of silence.

The Canticle of Zechariah may be recited or sung (page 114).

Then intercessions are made. If appropriate, all may respond to each intercession: "Lord, have mercy," or "Lord, hear our prayer." Examples of prayers of intercession are found on page 101 and following.

Then the Lord's Prayer is recited or sung.

In conclusion make the sign of the cross and say:

May the Lord bless us,
protect us from all evil,
and bring us to everlasting life.
Amen.

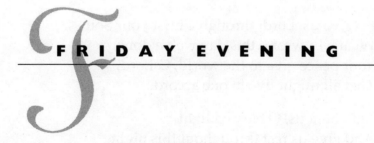

FRIDAY EVENING

After lighting a candle (if possible), make the sign of the cross and say:

God, come to my assistance.
Lord, make haste to me.

This hymn or another hymn is sung.

All praise to you, O God, this night,
For all the blessings of the light;
Keep us, we pray, O king of kings,
Beneath your own almighty wings.

Forgive us, Lord, through Christ your Son
Whatever wrong this day we've done;
Your peace give to the world, O Lord,
That all might live in one accord.

Enlighten us, O blessed light,
And give us rest throughout this night.
O strengthen us, that for your sake,
We all may serve you when we wake.

Psalm 121

If I look to the mountains,
will they come to my aid?
My help is the Lord,
who made earth and the heavens.

May God, ever wakeful,
keep you from stumbling;
the guardian of Israel
neither rests nor sleeps.

God shields you,
a protector by your side.
The sun shall not harm you by day
nor the moon at night.

God shelters you from evil,
securing your life.
God watches over you near and far,
now and always.

Let us pray.

After a time of silence:

Israel's guardian and Israel's helper,
will you still guard, still help?
Whatever our travels, travel with us.
Whatever our rest, rest beside us.
Lead us not into temptation,
deliver us from evil.
You are Lord for ever and ever.
Amen.

A passage from scripture may be read here, followed by a time of silence.

The Canticle of Mary may be recited or sung (page 116).

Then intercessions are made. If appropriate, all may respond to each intercession: "Lord, have mercy," or "Lord, hear our prayer." Examples of prayers of intercession are found on page 101 and following.

Then the Lord's Prayer is recited or sung.

Make the sign of the cross and say:

May the Lord bless us,
protect us from all evil,
and bring us to everlasting life.
Amen.

SATURDAY MORNING

Make the sign of the cross and say:

Lord, open my lips.
And my mouth will proclaim your praise.

This hymn or another hymn is sung.

Now that the daylight fills the sky,
We lift our hearts to God on high,
That God in all we do or say,
Would keep us free from harm today.

O Lord, restrain our tongues from strife,
From wrath and anger shield our life;
And guard with watchful care our eyes
That we will choose from all that's wise.

All praise to God the Father be,
And praise the Son eternally,
Whom with the Spirit we adore,
One God alone, for evermore.

Psalm 8

Lord our God,
the whole world tells
the greatness of your name.
Your glory reaches
beyond the stars.

Even the babble of infants
declares your strength,
your power to halt
the enemy and avenger.

I see your handiwork
in the heavens:
the moon and the stars
you set in place.

What is humankind
that you remember them,
the human race
that you care for them?

You treat them like gods,
dressing them in glory and splendor.
You give them charge of the earth,
laying all at their feet:

cattle and sheep,
wild beasts,
birds of the sky,
fish of the sea,
every swimming creature.

Lord our God,
the whole world tells
the greatness of your name.

Let us pray.

After a time of silence:

Rarely do we hear, O God,
those songs creation sings with you.
Our children and the childlike catch the tune,
but we who take charge of earth
have ears sealed by haste,
lips sealed by spilling words.
Remember us.
Remember us, Lord, that we may with right humility
befriend everything you have made
and so sing praise with all creation
for ever and ever.
Amen.

A passage from scripture may be read here, followed by a time of silence.

The Canticle of Zechariah may be recited or sung (page 114).

Then intercessions are made. If appropriate, all may respond to each intercession: "Lord, have mercy," or "Lord, hear our prayer." Examples of prayers of intercession are found on page 101 and following.

Then the Lord's Prayer is recited or sung.

In conclusion make the sign of the cross and say:

May the Lord bless us,
protect us from all evil,
and bring us to everlasting life.
Amen.

SATURDAY EVENING

The prayer of Saturday evening is the beginning of the prayers of Sunday, the Lord's Day.

After lighting a candle (if possible), make the sign of the cross and say:

God, come to my assistance.
Lord, make haste to me.

This hymn or another hymn is sung.

O blessed light, O Trinity,
O flowing source of unity,
The sun now sinks and burns the sky,
Bring light and grace lest hope should die.

In song we offer praise at dawn,
And pray when evening's cares are done.
With you, our glory, you, our praise,
May we sing humbly all our days.

To God the Father may there be
All glory, praise and majesty,
As in the Spirit with the Son
God lives and reigns for ever one.

Psalm 16

Protect me, God,
I turn to you for help.
I profess, "You are my Lord,
my greatest good."

I once put faith in false gods,
the idols of the land.
Now I make no offering to them,
nor invoke their names.
Those who chase after them
add grief upon grief.

Lord, you measure out my portion,
the shape of my future;
you mark off the best place for me
to enjoy my inheritance.

I bless God who teaches me,
who schools my heart even at night.
I am sure God is here,
right beside me.
I cannot be shaken.

So my heart rejoices,
my body thrills with life,
my whole being rests secure.

You will not abandon me to Sheol,
nor send your faithful one to death.
You show me the road to life:
boundless joy, at your side for ever!

Let us pray.

After a time of silence:

We wait for the week's first day,
the day that is yours, Lord of all time.
May this Lord's Day find us firm

in renouncing the demands of all other gods.
May it find us at rest in you alone.
May Sunday find us rejoicing to be passing over,
by your amazing grace,
from every way of death
to life at your side for ever and ever.
Amen.

A passage from scripture may be read here, followed by a time of silence.

The Canticle of Mary may be recited or sung (page 116).

Then intercessions are made. If appropriate, all may respond to each intercession: "Lord, have mercy," or "Lord, hear our prayer." Examples of prayers of intercession are found on page 101 and following.

Then the Lord's Prayer is recited or sung.

Make the sign of the cross and say:

May the Lord bless us,
protect us from all evil,
and bring us to everlasting life.
Amen.

MIDDAY PRAYER

One of the following psalms is prayed.

Psalm 23

The Lord is my shepherd,
I need nothing more.
You give me rest in green meadows,
setting me near calm waters,
where you revive my spirit.

You guide me along sure paths,
you are true to your name.
Though I should walk in death's dark valley,
I fear no evil with you by my side,
your shepherd's staff to comfort me.

You spread a table before me,
as my foes look on.
You soothe my head with oil;
my cup is more than full.

Goodness and love will tend me
every day of my life.
I will dwell in the house of the Lord
as long as I shall live.

Psalm 119:105 – 112

Your word is a lamp for my steps,
a light for my path.
I have sworn firmly
to uphold your just rulings.

I have suffered so much,
give me the life you promise.
Receive, Lord, all that I say,
and teach me your wisdom.

Though danger stalks,
I will never forget your law.
Though the wicked set traps,
I will not stray from you.

Your laws are my heritage,
the joy of my heart for ever.
I am determined to obey
for a lasting reward.

Psalm 128

How good to revere the Lord,
to walk in God's path.

Your table rich from labor —
how good for you!
Your beloved, a fruitful vine
in the warmth of your home.

Like olive shoots,
children surround your table.
This is your blessing
when you revere the Lord.

May the Lord bless you from Zion!
May you see Jerusalem prosper
every day of your life.
May you see your children's children,
and on Israel, peace!

NIGHT PRAYER

Make the sign of the cross and say:

Protect us, Lord, as we stay awake;
watch over us as we sleep,
that, awake, we may keep watch with Christ,
and, asleep, rest in his peace.

This hymn or another hymn is sung:

All praise to you, O God, this night,
For all the blessings of the light;
Keep us, we pray, O king of kings,
Beneath your own almighty wings.

Forgive us, Lord, through Christ your Son
Whatever wrong this day we've done;
Your peace give to the world, O Lord,
That all might live in one accord.

Teach me to live that I may dread
The grave as little as my bed;
Teach me to die that so I may
Rise glorious on that final day.

One of these psalms, another appropriate psalm, or the
Canticle of Simeon is recited.

Psalm 131

Lord, I am not proud,
holding my head too high,
reaching beyond my grasp.

No, I am calm and tranquil
like a weaned child
resting in its mother's arms:
my whole being at rest.

Let Israel rest in the Lord,
now and for ever.

Psalm 134

Bless the Lord,
all who serve in God's house,
who stand watch
throughout the night.

Lift up your hands
in the holy place
and bless the Lord.

And may God,
the maker of earth and sky,
bless you from Zion.

Canticle of Simeon

Lord, let your servant
now die in peace,
for you kept your promise.

With my own eyes
I see the salvation
you prepared for all peoples:

a light of revelation for the Gentiles
and glory to your people Israel.

*One of the following or another brief text from scripture
is read.*

Hear, O Israel: The Lord is our God, the Lord alone. You
shall love the Lord your God with all your heart, and
with all your soul, and with all your might. Keep these
words that I am commanding you today in your heart.
Recite them to your children and talk about them when
you are at home and when you are away, when you lie
down and when you rise.

DEUTERONOMY 6:4 – 7

You, O Lord, are in the midst of us,
and we are called by your name;
do not forsake us!

JEREMIAH 14:9

The final prayer and blessing are recited.

Lord,
we beg you to visit this house
and banish from it
all the deadly power of the enemy.
May your holy angels dwell here
to keep us in peace,
and may your blessing be upon us always.
We ask this through Christ our Lord.
Amen.

Make the sign of the cross during the blessing:

May the all-powerful Lord
grant us a restful night
and a peaceful death.
Amen.

*Night prayer concludes with a prayer or song addressed to the
Blessed Virgin Mary.*

Hail, holy Queen, Mother of mercy,
hail, our life, our sweetness, and our hope.
To you we cry, the children of Eve;
to you we send up our sighs,
mourning and weeping in this land of exile.
Turn, then, most gracious advocate,
your eyes of mercy toward us;
lead us home at last
and show us the blessed fruit of your womb, Jesus:
O clement, O loving, O sweet Virgin Mary.

BLESSINGS AT TABLE

The prayers here can be used, perhaps with some part of morning or evening prayer, for blessings before and after meals.

Lord, the lover of life,
you feed the birds of the skies
and array the lilies of the field.
We bless you for all your creatures
and for the food we are about to receive.
We humbly pray that in your goodness
you will provide for our brothers and sisters
    who are hungry.
We ask this through Christ our Lord.
Amen.

God of all goodness,
through the breaking of bread together
you strengthen the bonds that unite us in love.
Bless us and these your gifts.
Grant that as we sit down together at table
    in joy and sincerity,
we may grow always closer in the bonds of love.
We ask this through Christ our Lord.
Amen.

May your gifts refresh us, O Lord,
and your grace give us strength.
Amen.

Lord, you feed every living thing.
We have eaten together at this table;
keep us in your love.
Give us true concern
for the least of our sisters and brothers,
so that as we gladly share our food with them,
we may also sit down together with them
at the table of the kingdom of heaven.
We ask this through Christ our Lord.
Amen.

Lord, you have fed us from your gifts and favors;
fill us with your mercy,
for you live and reign for ever and ever.
Amen.

INTERCESSIONS

At morning prayer:

Christ, the sun of justice, dawns upon this new day.
We welcome with praise our unfailing light.
    Christ, true light, hear our prayer.

Rise again in glory,
that the hearts of all who preach your word
    may be set afire.
    Christ, true light, hear our prayer.

Show forth your splendor in the lives of the afflicted,
that the nations may hope in your promise.
    Christ, true light, hear our prayer.

Dawn with new radiance in the hearts of your disciples,
that we may be one with you in mind and heart.
    Christ, true light, hear our prayer.

Unveil the brightness of your wisdom in our work,
that the earth may be brought to fulfillment
in your image.
Christ, true light, hear our prayer.

Shine through the darkness which separates us
from each other,
that the human family may rejoice in true freedom.
Christ, true light, hear our prayer.

Give us eyes to see the beauty which surrounds us,
that our lives may be a living sacrifice of praise.
Christ, true light, hear our prayer.

Alternative intercessions for morning prayer:

Lord Jesus Christ, dawn from on high and
   creation's goal:

   Lord, have mercy.

Lord Jesus Christ, model for the church
   in service to the world:

Lord Jesus Christ, voice that calls the world to peace:

Lord Jesus Christ, constant help in daily life:

Lord Jesus Christ, healing hand and source of life:

Lord Jesus Christ, the word who speaks hope
   to the sick:

Lord Jesus Christ, strength of those oppressed
   by fear and need:

Lord Jesus Christ, hope of the dying and rest
   for the dead:

At evening prayer:

In peace, let us pray to the Lord.

   Lord, have mercy.

For the peace of the world, that a spirit of respect and forbearance may grow among peoples, let us pray to the Lord.

For the holy church of God, that it may be filled with truth and love, let us pray to the Lord.

For those in positions of public trust, that they may serve justice and promote the dignity and freedom of all people, let us pray to the Lord.

For a blessing upon the labors of all, and for the right use of the riches of creation, let us pray to the Lord.

For the poor, the persecuted, the sick, and all who suffer; for refugees, prisoners and those in danger, let us pray to the Lord.

For our congregation, that we may be delivered from hardness of heart and show forth God's glory in all that we do, let us pray to the Lord.

For our enemies and those who wish us harm and for all whom we have injured or offended, let us pray to the Lord.

For the forgiveness of our sins and for the grace of the Holy Spirit to amend our lives, let us pray to the Lord.

For our families, friends and neighbors, let us pray to the Lord.

For all who have died, that with all the saints they may have rest, let us pray to the Lord.

Alternative intercessions for evening prayer:

In peace, let us pray to the Lord.

  Lord, have mercy.

For an evening that is perfect, holy, peaceful and without sin, let us pray to the Lord.

For an angel of peace, a faithful guide and guardian of our souls and bodies, let us pray to the Lord.

For the pardon and forgiveness of our sins and offenses, let us pray to the Lord.

For the holy church of God, that God may give it peace and unity and protect it throughout the whole world, let us pray to the Lord.

For this city and for every city and country and all living in them, let us pray to the Lord.

For seasonable weather, bountiful harvests and for peaceful times, let us pray to the Lord.

For the safety of travelers, the recovery of the sick, the deliverance of the oppressed and the release of captives, let us pray to the Lord.

For all that is good and profitable to our souls and for the peace of the world, let us pray to the Lord.

For a peaceful and Christian end to our lives without shame or pain, and for a good defense before the awesome judgment seat of Christ, let us pray to the Lord.

In the communion of the Holy Spirit and of all the saints, let us commend ourselves and one another to the living God through Christ our Lord.

At morning or evening prayer during Advent:

Ageless Wisdom, come and guide your people.
Reveal to us the splendor of your truth.
    Radiant Lord, prepare our hearts for your coming.

Lord of history, come and reveal God's plan for us.
Free us to journey toward the advent we celebrate.
    Radiant Lord, prepare our hearts for your coming.

Blossom and yield from the root of Jesse,
come and bless our days.
Gather to one banquet table all who seek
    God's holy face.
    Radiant Lord, prepare our hearts for your coming.

Offspring of David, come and turn our hearts.
Fling open the gates that imprison the just
and that oppress the poor.
    Radiant Lord, prepare our hearts for your coming.

Light from the East, come and shine upon us.
Rise up in glory for those in the shadow of despair
and grief.
   Radiant Lord, prepare our hearts for your coming.

Savior of the nations, come and heal us.
Destroy the weapons of hatred that divide us
and establish the world in your reign of peace.
   Radiant Lord, prepare our hearts for your coming.

Unfailing presence, come and draw us to yourself.
Bring into the fullness of your glory all who have died.
   Radiant Lord, prepare our hearts for your coming.

At morning and evening prayer during Lent:

Let us bless the name of Jesus,
the light and guide of our lenten passage.
  Lord, by your love set us free.

Word of God in our flesh,
guide our vision and bend us to your will.
  Lord, by your love set us free.

Bread of affliction,
turn our fasting into a desire for your presence.
  Lord, by your love set us free.

Remedy for Satan's empty promises,
strengthen us in our lenten prayer.
  Lord, by your love set us free.

Beloved child and true servant of God,
confirm in love the church you have called forth.
  Lord, by your love set us free.

Treasury of wisdom,
give insight to all marked by your cross.
  Lord, by your love set us free.

Faithful witness,
destroy the idols which keep us from dying with you.
  Lord, by your love set us free.

At morning and evening prayer during Easter:

Bridegroom of the church,
bring to perfection those assembled to sing your praise.
    Risen Lord, rule our hearts.

Wellspring of all holiness,
fashion in your image a people of hope.
    Risen Lord, rule our hearts.

Architect of the New Jerusalem,
lead all people into God's radiant light.
    Risen Lord, rule our hearts.

Temple of God's presence,
calm all our fears in this season of your victory.
    Risen Lord, rule our hearts.

Cornerstone of the new creation,
build up your church in the service of the poor.
    Risen Lord, rule our hearts.

MORNING: Canticle of Zechariah

Praise the Lord, the God of Israel,
who shepherds the people and sets them free.

God raises from David's house
a child with power to save.
Through the holy prophets
God promised in ages past
to save us from enemy hands,
from the grip of all who hate us.

The Lord favored our ancestors
recalling the sacred covenant,
the pledge to our ancestor Abraham,
to free us from our enemies,
so we might worship without fear
and be holy and just all our days.

And you, child, will be called
Prophet of the Most High,
for you will come to prepare
a pathway for the Lord
by teaching the people salvation
through forgiveness of their sin.

Out of God's deepest mercy
a dawn will come from on high,
light for those shadowed by death,
a guide for our feet on the way to peace.

LUKE 1:68 – 79

CANTICLE OF ZECHARIAH

EVENING: Canticle of Mary

I acclaim the greatness of the Lord,
I delight in God my savior,
who regarded my humble state.
Truly from this day on
all ages will call me blest.

For God, wonderful in power,
has used that strength for me.
Holy the name of the Lord!
whose mercy embraces the faithful,
one generation to the next.

The mighty arm of God
scatters the proud in their conceit,
pulls tyrants from their thrones,
and raises up the humble.
The Lord fills the starving
and lets the rich go hungry.

God rescues lowly Israel,
recalling the promise of mercy,
the promise made to our ancestors,
to Abraham's heirs for ever.

LUKE 1:46 – 55

Endnotes

On this day the first of days: Trans. by Henry William Baker, 1821 – 1877, Hymns Ancient and Modern. Reproduced by permission.

O radiant light: © William Storey.

Now that daylight fills the sky: From *Hymnal for the Hours,* © 1989, GIA Publications, Inc. Chicago IL.

O splendor of eternal light: © Gethsemani Abbey.

Great Lord of splendor: © Gethsemani Abbey.

Lord Jesus Christ, abide with us: © St. Joseph's Abbey, Spencer MA.

We praise you, Father: © Malling Abbey, West Malling, Kent, England.

Awake, be lifted up, O heart: From *Hymnal for the Hours,* © 1989, GIA Publications, Inc. Chicago IL.

We bless you, Father, Lord of life: © Stanbrook Abbey 1974.

All praise to you, O God, this night: From *Hymnal for the Hours,* © 1989, GIA Publications, Inc. Chicago IL.

O blessed light: © 1989 by GIA Publications, Inc. Chicago IL. All rights reserved.